First World War
and Army of Occupation
War Diary
France, Belgium and Germany

25 DIVISION
74 Infantry Brigade
Sherwood Foresters
(Nottinghamshire and Derbyshire Regiment)
1/7th Battalion
1 September 1918 - 28 February 1919

WO95/2247/4

The Naval & Military Press Ltd
www.nmarchive.com
Published in association with The National Archives

Published by

The Naval & Military Press Ltd

Unit 10 Ridgewood Industrial Park,

Uckfield, East Sussex,

TN22 5QE England

Tel: +44 (0) 1825 749494

www.naval-military-press.com

www.nmarchive.com

This diary has been reprinted in facsimile from the original. Any imperfections are inevitably reproduced and the quality may fall short of modern type and cartographic standards.

© Crown Copyright
Images reproduced by permission of The National Archives, London, England, 2015.

Contents

Document type	Place/Title	Date From	Date To
Document type	**Place/Title**	**Date From**	**Date To**
Heading	WO95/2247-5		
Heading	11th Bn Notts & Derby Regt (Sherwood Foresters) Sep 1918-Feb 1919		
Heading	War Diary September 1918 11th Bn Sherwood Foresters		
War Diary	Front Trenches Left Battn of British Front Asiago Plateau	01/09/1918	01/09/1918
War Diary	Same Place	01/09/1918	03/09/1918
War Diary	Serona Camp West	04/09/1918	08/09/1918
War Diary	Serona Camp West Asiago Plateau	08/09/1918	11/09/1918
War Diary	Centrale	11/09/1918	13/09/1918
War Diary	In The Train	14/09/1918	18/09/1918
War Diary	Coulonvillers France	19/09/1918	27/09/1918
War Diary	Heilly	28/09/1918	29/09/1918
War Diary	Maricourt	30/09/1918	30/09/1918
Heading	War Diary Sheets 1 to 22 October 1918		
War Diary	Maricourt	01/10/1918	02/10/1918
War Diary	Moislains	03/10/1918	03/10/1918
War Diary	Mt St Martin	03/10/1918	11/10/1918
War Diary	Honnecchy	12/10/1918	12/10/1918
War Diary	Premont	13/10/1918	21/10/1918
War Diary	Honnechy	22/10/1918	31/10/1918
Miscellaneous	Addenda		
War Diary	Pommereuil	01/11/1918	04/11/1918
War Diary	Fair De France	04/11/1918	05/11/1918
War Diary	Maroilles	05/11/1918	06/11/1918
War Diary	Marbaix	07/11/1918	07/11/1918
War Diary	Maroilles	08/11/1918	08/11/1918
War Diary	Bousies	09/11/1918	13/11/1918
War Diary	Le Cateau	14/11/1918	29/11/1918
War Diary	St Hilaire	29/11/1918	29/12/1918
War Diary	Louvignies Sheet Valenniecinnes 1/100,000	30/12/1918	31/12/1918
War Diary	Louvignies Les Quesnoy Valenciennes (Sheet 1/100,000)	01/01/1919	21/01/1919
War Diary	Louvignies	21/01/1919	31/01/1919
War Diary	Louvignies Les Quesnoy (Valenciennes Sheet)	01/02/1919	13/02/1919
War Diary	Louvignies	13/02/1919	17/02/1919
War Diary	Sheet 51A	18/02/1919	28/02/1919

WO95/22475

25TH DIVISION
74TH INFY BDE

11TH BN NOTTS & DERBY REGT
(SHERWOOD FORESTERS)
SEP 1918 - FEB 1919

from 23 DIV. 70 Bde
and ITALY SAME DIV

WAR DIARY
or
INTELLIGENCE SUMMARY

(Erase heading not required.)

Army Form C. 2118.

War Diary — September 1918
11th Bn. Sherwood Foresters

Vol 36

Army Form C. 2118.

Page 31

WAR DIARY
INTELLIGENCE SUMMARY

(Erase heading not required.) 11th Bn Sherwood Foresters

Instructions regarding War Diaries and Intelligence Summaries are contained in F.S. Regs., Part II. and the Staff Manual respectively. Title Pages September will be prepared in manuscript.

Place	Date	Hour	Summary of Events and Information	Remarks and references to Appendices
Front trenches Left Battn of British Front ASIAGO PLATEAU	Sept 1st		Battalion still holding the front line from TRAVERSO on its West, with the Italians (BERSAGLIERI Regt.) carried on the line to the West, to a point immediately North of PERGHELE on the right. The front line running approximately along the southern edge of the Gorge of the GHELPAC. Strong rumours of the imminent retirement of the Austrian line to the Northern edge of the ASIAGO PLATEAU with its line running along COSTA - BOSCO - NETTE - and thence along the Northern edge of the VAL D'ASSA), kept most prevalent. In case of such a retirement the Division was to take up an outpost line along the line CROCE - CANOVE - CANOVE DI SOTTO - and thence to the high ground between the VAL D'ASSA on the North and the GHELPAC on the South. The Battalion being ordered to occupy as an outpost line the enemy front line from STELLA (about 700 yards West of CANOVE DI SOTTO) through AMBROSINI. The trench strength of the Battalion at the commencement of September was 17 officers and 560 ORs - the ration strength was 14 officers and 670 ORs and 72 horses.	

Army Form C. 2118.

WAR DIARY
INTELLIGENCE SUMMARY
(Erase heading not required.)

September 1918.   11th Bn. Sherwood Foresters

Page 3.

Place	Date	Hour	Summary of Events and Information	Remarks and references to Appendices
Same place	1st		Four strong reconnoitring patrols, each of strength 1 officer & 30 O.Rs. had been sent out, two at a time during the night, endeavouring to discover the enemy's dispositions. Preparation made by C.Coy. (Lieut (Platoon) most (often Gp¹⁸ South) for the night Sept: 2/3. Strong reconnoitring patrols again sent out — the enemy were apparently still holding the front line. The proposed raid was cancelled, and a	
do.	2		Strong offensive patrol of 2 officers & 30 O.Rs. was sent out at 11 p.m. to endeavour to enter & occupy the enemy front line at AMBROS.N.1. 2ⁿᵈ Lieut. W.H.Mc. HOTSON was in command and carried out an excellent patrol but was unable to effect his object, owing to M.G., rifle fire and L.T.M. and bombs. The patrol having returned without casualties after having thoroughly woken up the enemy causing them to fire numerous white and red very lights. Captain T.H. SPICER, having been recalled from leave reported at B. Echelon, CAMISINO. 2ⁿᵈ Lieut. N.E. SWIRE, M.C. returned from hospital & & and reported to C Coy in the line on the 2ⁿᵈ.	
do.	3		The Battalion was relieved by the 11th West Yorkshire Regt. and on relief moved to SERONA CAMP West, becoming a Battalion of the	

WAR DIARY
INTELLIGENCE SUMMARY

11th Bn. Sherwood Foresters

September 1918.

Place	Date	Hour	Summary of Events and Information	Remarks and references to Appendices
	3rd		Brigade in Divisional Reserve. Relief was complete by 1.30 a.m. Rev. G. BARNSLEY, C.F. reported to the Battalion and was taken on the attached strength as Chaplain. The following extract appeared in the London Gazette dated Aug. 27th 1918 – Notts & Derby Regt. Temp. Lieut. O.R. ORCHARD from M.G.C. (Inf.) to be temp. Lieut. (June 13th with Seniority Oct. 1st 1916.) 2nd Lieut. T. HODSON (attd. 70th Batt. M.G.) proceeded to CAMBRIDGE Sept. 1st to attend an Adjutants' Course commencing Sept. 6th	
SERONA Camp Beart.	4th		Interior economy and generally clearing up. Captain J.H. SPICER re-assumed command of D Coy. Captain R.W. CLARK, M.C., took over command + part of B Coy from 2nd Lt. (a/Captain) H.A. WATTS, who re-assumed the appointment of Asst. Adjt.	
do.	5th		Company training and interior economy. 9 O.R's rejoined from the G.H.Q. Reinforcement Camps. Sgt. (a/C.S.M.) S. Thompson, C Coy. was confirmed in the rank of Coy. Sgt. Major with effect from 9.8.1918. Lieut. F.W.K. LAWRIE, R.A.M.C., 2nd Lieut. W.A. POWELL and 5 O.R's rejoined	

WAR DIARY

Army Form C. 2118.

Page 34.

INTELLIGENCE SUMMARY

September 1918.   11th Bn. Sherwood Foresters

Place	Date	Hour	Summary of Events and Information	Remarks and references to Appendices
SERONA Camp Bent	5th		from leave to the U.K.	
do.	6th		Company training. 2/Captain W.A. CLIFTON, MC, having been recalled from leave to the U.K, reported for duty.	
do.	7th		Company training. Lieut. D.R. ORCHARD, 2nd Lt. T. CHEETHAM, MC, 2nd Lt. CH. ROSE reported from General, Signalling & Scouting Courses respectively. 2nd Lt. T. CHEETHAM, MC, appointed Anti. Aircraft. Offr. vice 2nd Lt. & a/Capt. H.A. WATTS, who returns to duty with B Coy. 2nd Lt. effect from 9.9.1918. On instructions received from the 70th Bde. a scheme for a raid was drawn up and approved by the Bde. & Div. Cmdrs. All details were kept secret from everyone except Captain P.H. GIBSON, MC, and Staff Sergt. Cmdr. R.A. meanwhile training (intensive) was carried on, camouflaged as if a general advance owing to the rumoured retirement of the Austrians, which had been on the tapis for some time.	SF 4119/142 atchd.
do.	8th		Church parade arranged so as not to interfere with training as above. All officers & platoon Sgts, who were to partake in the raid, were taken to an O.P. in the forward area so as to view the scene of the raid. These were all front under their moral of secrecy not to tell	

Army Form C. 2118.

WAR DIARY
or
INTELLIGENCE SUMMARY.
(Erase heading not required.)

11th Bn. Sherwood Foresters

Page 38.

September 1918

Place	Date	Hour	Summary of Events and Information	Remarks and references to Appendices
Serena Camp West ASIAGO PLATEAU	Sept 8	Out Control	Anyone about whom they had been or for what reason - meanwhile orders were issued for the attack 2 Coy (A+B) to be ready to go round the line in the afternoon, but this order was subsequently postponed until the following morning.	
do	9th		Major J. Abbey, DSO, MC, RA, explained the Artillery Scheme of the Raid to C+D Coy, to whom full details were now given for the first time. The Artillery Barrage included: Nine 6" Batteries (20 guns) H- 6" heavl mortars, six field batteries 18 hrowitzers (36 guns) Six 4.5" Howitzer batteries, 18 strokes mortars. Barrage 60% H.E. + 40% Shrapnel. In addition to these protecting guns, the field guns fired a intense neutralisation fire was carried out on battery positions known enemy targets. The following awards were afterwards given for this Raid and the villains were presented by Brig. Gen. H. Baker, CMG, DSO on the 13th Sept.	Report on action. SF awg/3 dated 13/9/18.
			Captain P.H. Gibson MC — Bar to MC	DCM C Coy
			2nd Lt + a/Capt. J.H. Spier — MC	
			2nd Lt. R.J. Charlton — MC	
			2nd Lt. W.P. Bramber — MC	
			15739 Sgt. C. Robinson MM — Bar to MM	DCM C Coy
			269819 Pte J. Pope —	DCM D Coy
			1496 Pte. E. Scott MM — Bar to MM and promoted Cpl. to fill the first vacancy.	C Coy

Army Form C. 2118.

Page 36

WAR DIARY
INTELLIGENCE SUMMARY.
(Erase heading not required.)

11th Bn. Shorwood Foresters

Place	Date	Hour	Summary of Events and Information	Remarks and references to Appendices
Serona Court West ASIAGO PLATEAU	September 1918 9th Contd.		241184 Pte J. Gore C Coy — M.M. 29836 Pte W. Batchford D Coy — MM. 72084 Pte A. Rainey D Coy — MM. 240855 Pte E. Pearson C Coy — MM. 16024 Pte A. Cheshley HQ'd Coy — MM 305249 L/Sgt. H. Wardale D Coy — MM 28461 Pte H. Cochran D Coy — MM (Authority:- AMS.[ITAY] H.R. 271 dated 11.9.1918 & 23rd DRO. 475 of 13.9.18.) The following names were also submitted with reference to this raid 73199 Pte J. Sutherland C Coy 6674 Cpl. J. W. Clarke MM. C Coy 17957 Sgt. E. Antcliffe SCM.MM. D Coy 17905 Pte S. Smith C Coy 305649 Sgt. G. Johnson C Coy 11359 CSM. S. Thompson (F) C Coy Mention unfortunately was omitted in the official report of the perfect way in which the men moved up to the various enemy positions under the cover of our own barrage, & this was was the probable reason why our casualties were so slight although a large number of the enemy were killed. Not a little of the success of the raid is probably due to the excellent patrol work made by Lt. W.H.McI. Hotson during the 2 days last prior in the line which ended on the 3rd Sept, add also # to the bravery & good leadership displayed by him during the raid itself. The success of the raid being only marred by the	

WAR DIARY
or
INTELLIGENCE SUMMARY

Army Form C. 2118.

Page 37

1/1st Sherwood Foresters

September 1918.

Place	Date	Hour	Summary of Events and Information	Remarks and references to Appendices
Siena Camp West ASIAGO PLATEAU.	9th Contd.		unfortunate death caused by a stray bullet, when the Band was practically over & the Coys. were withdrawing to our lines.	
do.	10th		Orders were received and moved for the Battn. to move into CARRIOLA CAMP where it would become the Reserve Battn. Rgtl Bde. Wire was received from General Babington Cmdg 23rd Division saying "Well done", and also one from Col. Whitford Cmdg 69th Bde, saying "Hearty congratulations on your Raid from all ranks of the 69th Bde." Orders received cancelling the Bde. Orders regarding the move of the Battn. as above. 8am. Col. Young ordered to attend a Conference at Bde HQ.	
do.	11th	3am.		
		10.30 am	During his absence, orders received from Bde telephono messages & fragmentary were received for the Bn. to move to CENTRALE. By 12 midday. Bn HQ. had moved off and the remaining Coys. following; the CO. returning about 12.15pm. finding the tail of the Bn. leaving camp. Major Smalley Rent. 2nd in Comd. R.S.M. Richland & about 20 men were left behind to clear up the camp & hand it over to the Rhea Cracks. The Battn. marched down the mule track arriving at CENTRALE CAMP about 5.30pm. The CO. & Adjt. visited B Echelon at convisano which also moved to CENTRALE, this move not being completed until	

WAR DIARY
INTELLIGENCE SUMMARY

Page 38.
Army Form C. 2118.

11th Bn. Sherwood Foresters
September 1918

Place	Date	Hour	Summary of Events and Information	Remarks and references to Appendices
CENTALE	11th	Contd	about 3 am on the following day, the 9th YORKSHIRE Regt under Lt Col. R.S. HART, DSO (Sherwood Foresters) from the 69th Bde & the 13th D.L.I. under Lt. Col. D.H. CLARKE, DSO, MC (Baby Clarke) from the 68th Bde were also in the Camp & had received similar orders. Lieut. S.E. McC. KENDALL reported from Hospital & attached to A Coy for duty. 2nd Lt. G.W. GIMBER admitted to hospital.	
do.	12th		The Bn. paraded with the 9th Yorks & 13th D.L.I. at 10 a.m. when Brig. Gen. BYRON (CRA 23rd Div.) read out Maj. Gen. Sir J. Babington's Farewell Speech. Afterwards Brig. Gen. H. GORDON, CMG, DSO, presented ribbons as mentioned above (Sept 9.27) and said "Good-bye" to the Battalion. "For he's a jolly good fellow" was spontaneously sung by the men & three hearty cheers given for the Brigadier. C & D Coys were to have entrained at 1.30 am & A & B Coys at 7 am on the following day, but at 10.30 pm three hams were postponed by the Station Railway Authorities. Captain R.H. Field rejoined the Bn. from hospital but was re-admitted on the following day. Major E. Smalley, DSO, proceeded to ENGLAND as Instructor. Captain R.H. Green, MC, was attached off the strength (attached) & assumed the duties of Legal in command. Men who were on attachment to Division Hd. Bde. rejoined the Battalion	

WAR DIARY
INTELLIGENCE SUMMARY

Army Form C. 2118.

Page 39.

11th Bn. Sherwood Foresters

September 1918.

Place	Date	Hour	Summary of Events and Information	Remarks and references to Appendices
CENTRALE	13th		Reveille 5.30am, bivouacs were struck & the Bn. marched out at 6.30am moving to a field adjoining MORANO station, where bivouacs were again pitched & the Bn. stayed there for the day, awaiting entrainment orders. C & D Coys under Captain R.L. Eborn M.C. entrained during the evening & the train moved off at 8pm — strength on the train was — 12 officers 397 ORs & 30 horses. A & B Coys under the CO entrained shortly afterwards & departed at 11.30pm — strength on this train; 9 officers 367 ORs, 23 horses. Passed VICENZA & PADOVA during the night.	
In the train	14th		Halted at 7.30am for 1½ hours at BOLOGNA - passed through PARMA, PIACENZA, STRADELLA, VOGHERA (5.30pm Halt 2 hrs), TORTONA & ARQUATA. Captain C.W. BARTLETT M.C. rejoined from hospital at ARQUATA. Passed through GENOA & SAVONA during the night & reached the Italian Riviera in the early morning. At 10 am the frontier at VENTIMILLE was crossed. The following places were passed during the morning — MENTONE, MONTE CARLO, MONACO, NICE & ANTIBES and a halt of 5 hours was made at CANNES, where the majority of the Bn. had a bathe. TOULON, MARSEILLES and AVIGNON were passed during the evening & night.	
do.	15th			

Army Form C. 2118.

WAR DIARY
INTELLIGENCE SUMMARY.
(Erase heading not required.)

Page 40.

11/NF. Sherwood Foresters.

September 1918.

Place	Date	Hour	Summary of Events and Information	Remarks and references to Appendices
In the train	16th		At 6 am a halt upon was made at ORANGE, and the journey was continued along the RHONE VALLEY, passing through VALENCE, LYONS, MACON, CHALON and DIJON.	
do	17th		The journey was continued but the travelling was rather slower. PARIS was circumvented during the evening and AMIENS passed in the night.	
do	18th		ABBEVILLE was reached at 5 am & ST. RIQUIER at 6 am where the Battn. detrained & marched to billets at COULONVILLERS. The Battn. then became a Battalion of the 7th Inf. Bde. commanded by Brig. Gen. H.M. CRAIGIE-HALKETT DSO, the other two Battns. of the Bde. being the 9 H. L. I. & 13th D.L.I. The remaining Brigades of the 25th Division commanded by Maj. Gen. CHARLES, CB, DSO, were the 74th Bde. commanded by Brig. Gen. —— and the 75th Bde. commanded by Brig. Gen. ——	
COULONVILLERS FRANCE	19th		Cleaning up etc. in billets. The Battn. was inspected by B.C. M. CRAIGIE-HALKETT, DSO, who expressed himself pleased with the appearance of the men & also gave them a welcome to the 25th Division on behalf of area in ITALY	

F.H. FRITH + Lt. Col. G.W. GIMBER

WAR DIARY
or INTELLIGENCE SUMMARY

Army Form C. 2118.

Page 41

11th Bn. Sherwood Foresters
September 1918.

Place	Date	Hour	Summary of Events and Information	Remarks and references to Appendices
COUIN VILLERS	19th Contd.		and struck off the strength. 2nd Lieut. E.F.L. THOMPSON, A.S.C., evacuated sick out of the Divl. area in Italy & struck off the attd. strength.	
do.	20th		Company training. The following extracts from the London Gazette were published in Bn.Os. Sept. 9th – Temp. Captain R.S. 2nd M.C. to be Actg. Capt. (March 19th) Lt. Daley. Sept. 17th – Temp. 2nd Lieut. W.A. CLIFTON M.C. to be Acting Captain whilst Cmdg. a Coy. (June 30th).	
do.	21st		Company training. 2nd Lt. T. Cheetham appointed Bn. Signalling Officer. 2nd Lt. C.H. Rose appointed Asst. Adjt. vice 2nd Lt. L. Cheetham M.C.	
do.	22nd		Church parade. The G.O.C. 25th Division approved the T/Captain R.H. Eskor M.C. wearing the badges of rank of Major whilst employed as 2nd in Command (authority 25th Div. A 67 dated 20.9.1918.)	
do.	23rd		Company training. Staff note number the Div. Commander, Maj. Gen. Charles C.B. D.S.O. in the afternoon. The C.O., 2nd in Command, Adjt. & Capt. Bartlett attended.	
do.	24th		Company in attack practice. A warning was received to prepare to move at short notice. 2nd Lieut. J.R. Pamfrey of the Rgt. attached to the Battn. to take over temporarily the duties of Transport officer vice 2nd Lieut. W.R. Garrett who returned to duty with B Coy. In accordance with	

Page 42

WAR DIARY
INTELLIGENCE SUMMARY

Army Form C. 2118.

11th Bn. Sherwood Foresters

September 1918.

Place	Date	Hour	Summary of Events and Information	Remarks
COULONVILLERS	24th		Verbal instructions received from the B.E.C., Lieut. A. Munchie was attached to the 9th Yorkshire Regt.	
do.	25th		Company training. The transport less cookers, baggage wagons, mess cart & watercart moved off by stages taking 3 days to the HEILLY area. Battalion in attack practice during the morning. Preparations for the move on the following day.	
do.	26th			
do.	27th		Marched from COULONVILLERS to ST. REQUIER, where the Battalion entrained about 2pm. ALBERT was reached about 8.30pm and the Bn. marched to LILLE at HEILLY arriving about 11.30pm, the remainder of the transport entrained at PONT REMY and arrived at HEILLY during the early morning.	
HEILLY	28th		Battalion in the attack tactics in the afternoon. A warning order was received to be prepared to move to a forward area the following day.	
HEILLY	29th		The transport moved by marched route to MARICOURT moving off at 6 a.m. The Battalion embussed on the AMIENS-ALBERT ROAD at 11 a.m. and arrived at MARICOURT during the afternoon, occupying an old camp, which had been rather knocked about.	

WAR DIARY
INTELLIGENCE SUMMARY

(Erase heading not required.)

Army Form C. 2118.

Page 43

Title pages _September 1918_ 11th Bn. Sherwood Foresters

Place	Date	Hour	Summary of Events and Information	Remarks and references to Appendices
MARICOURT	Sept 30th		The Battalion took part in a Brigade in attack during the morning, marching towards COMBLES. Major P.H. Gilson M.C. took over Command of the Battalion vice Lt. Col. Young (auth 74th Feb. G.13.04 29.9.1918) Lt.Col. H.N. Young DSO took over temporary command of the 75th Bde (auth 74th Bde G.13.04 29.9.1918). Information was received that Lt. Col. C.F. Hudson VC. DSO. MC., who had arrived in France, had been posted to a Regular Battn. + would not return to the Battn. It was afterwards heard that he had been given the acting Command of the 2 Bn. Sherwood Foresters. The following extracts from the London Gazette were published in BOs. Sept. 23rd P.E. McC. Kemball relinquishes the Act. Rank of Captain (additional) June 8th Temp. 2nd Lieut. J.H. Spicer to be temp. Lieut (acting Captain) September 15. 2nd Lieut. V.C. Smith admitted to hospital 29.9.1918. Made preparations to move to MOISLAINS on the following day.	

A. N. Young
Lieut. Colonel
O/C 11th Bn. Sherwood Foresters

94/25

Army Form C. 2118.

WAR DIARY
or
INTELLIGENCE SUMMARY.
(Erase heading not required.)

April 37

War Diary

Feb 1 to 28

October 1916

M 37

Army Form C. 2118.

WAR DIARY
INTELLIGENCE SUMMARY.
(Erase heading not required.)

Sheet 1
1/8 Bn Sherwood Foresters

Place	Date	Hour	Summary of Events and Information	Remarks and references to Appendices
MARICOURT	Oct/1/18		The Battalion moved from MARICOURT to MOISLAINS	
	2nd		Remained at MOISLAINS	
MOISLAINS	3rd	1pm	The Battalion was advancing by during the morning and at 1pm moved out of camp on route for PONSSOY Turning the march, when news received that the stay at PONSSOY would only be half an hour or so which to have been cancelled the Brigade moved over to Mt ST MARTIN. "B" Echelon was left at MN 38.24. The Battalion took up its old trench positions at Mt. ST MARTIN. HQ Coy & "A" and two Coys per Coys were served out to every got out hot half ours Luncheon. Term sent back to "B" Echelon.	
Mt ST MARTIN NIGHT			He though of the fighting portion of the Battalion was 14 Officers & 691 ORs During the night 8/4 the arrangements for "A" Echelon were leaving. Lieut A D WHIFE, Lieut H GARRETT were appointed together with 2 OCs Kelledy Tornwell & J Allison. Zr Lieut J A RAMSEY attached 1/6 Battalion.	

WAR DIARY
or
INTELLIGENCE SUMMARY.

Army Form C. 2118.

Head 2
11 Batt the Durham Light Infantry

Place	Date	Hour	Summary of Events and Information	Remarks and references to Appendices
NR ST. MARTIN	3rd Cont.		Transport Officer from the 2/6 York & Lab came up from "B" Echelon with returns, a complete and missing together with the name in charge of the water cart who has fallen.	
NR ST MARTIN	4		During the course of the day the Battalion was standing by with the remainder of the Brigade in readiness to support the 4th Brigade (20 Division) who were advancing. At 09.00 hours orders were received stating that the Brigade would advance on a 3 Battalion frontage on the morning of 05.3.4. The 9 YORKS Regt on the right, the 13. D.L.I. in the Centre & the 11. S.L. on the left. The Brigade objective was a line running approximately from - the Centre of the Eastern outskirts of BEAUFORT & LA SABLONIERE (inclusive) & hence along the high ground to GUISANCOURT FARM (inclusive) the Battalion objective was N.O.E. edge of GUISANCOURT FARM (inclusive) to a point about 1,200 yards EAST along the high ground. The Division	

WAR DIARY
INTELLIGENCE SUMMARY

Army Form C. 2118

Sheet 3

1/4th Bn the Welchurnd Fusiliers

Place	Date	Hour	Summary of Events and Information	Remarks and references to Appendices
ST MARTIN	Oct 4th		Battalion was about 1500 yards in rear of assembly position about 1000 yards south of GUISNCOURT FARM and was in position by 0300 hours on the 5th.	
	Oct 5th		During the assembly hour 6E. M.C. members were slightly wounded. In the leg 2 3,003 were wounded by M.G. fire. Zero hour was 0600 hours up to which hour the barrage fired & the battalion advanced on its objective. 3 Coys in the line in order A B C from the right with D Coy in support. All objectives were gained with slighter opposition than was expected. Considering that the left flank had to move up to the MASNIERES - BEAUVOIR LINE of the big HINDENBURG defences, GUISNCOURT FARM being a strong point in the line was strongly held by machine guns. The Battalion objectives were reinforced by 0800 hours and consolidation begun. 1 Officer and 190 Germans were taken prisoners and a total of 3 officers and 300 the latter by the Division. A number of Germans were killed and wounded.	

WAR DIARY

INTELLIGENCE SUMMARY

Army Form C. 2118.

(Erase heading not required.)

Place: Boesinghe **Sheet** 4.
11th Bn. The Sherwood Foresters

Date	Hour	Summary of Events and Information	Remarks and references to Appendices
Oct 9 contd		My L/G rifles & men captured. The Battalion's left flank was always secure. PROSPECT HILL to the immediate West of S was not being captured by the 50th Division the way before. The 3rd D.L.I. however failed to make good their objective, with the result that the right flank of the Battalion was badly enfiladed from the high ground East of GUIENCOURT FARM and consequently at about 0830 hours had to fall back & form a defensive flank to link up with the right Battalion. This eventually necessitated a withdrawal to the Northern edge of GUISENCOURT FARM and a line was overgrown from there running in a S.E. direction towards BELLEVUE FARM and we consolidated. During this operation the casualties were:— 2nd Lt. W.N. BRANKER M.C. killed, 2nd Lt. M.W. POWELL killed (shell), Lieut (A/Capt) R.W. CLARK M.C. wounded by M.G. fire (leg broken), 2nd Lt. H.G. WHITTINGTON wounded by M.G. fire (leg & elbow broken), 2nd Lt. T. CHEETHAM M.C. wounded in arm by M.G. bullet. O.R.	

WAR DIARY
or
INTELLIGENCE SUMMARY

Army Form C. 2118.

Sheet 5.
11th Bn. The Warwick Regt.

Place	Date	Hour	Summary of Events and Information	Remarks and references to Appendices
	5 Oct		PREYTARD wounded at 14.45 by M.G. bullet (neck). Captain (A/Major) L.H. GIBSON, M.C. wounded at 18.45, M.G. bullet left forearm. 12 O.R.s Killed (including C.S.M. G. WILLIAMS, M.M.) 120 O.R.s wounded (including C.S.M. J. BETTS) 10 O.R.s missing & 2 died of wounds. At about 1600 hours two Companies 8 Warwicks (75th Brigade) were attached to the Battalion at 1615 hours one of these Coys took one platoon & the other Company re-attached GUISANCOURT FARM but remained under new Lewis M.G. fire from buildings of the farm went aimable to make any advance. No appreciable artillery was brought for the purpose. After nightfall about 2000 hours our line was again advanced about 200 yards on the right & consolidated. The left flank of the Battalion remained where it was, about 300 yds from the farm.	
	6		In accordance with orders received at 12.00 hours 5/Mount re-attached to its Battalion. For this attack the one two Companies 5/R. Warwicks and 2 platoons "A" Co. 11/R.	

Army Form C. 2118.

WAR DIARY
INTELLIGENCE SUMMARY.
(Erase heading not required.)

Sheet 6

1/7 Bn. the Sherwood Foresters

Place	Date	Hour	Summary of Events and Information	Remarks and references to Appendices
	Sept. 6th Oct.		Battalion on the 6th Inst. were attached to 5th Brigade. The Brigade objective was the same as for the 5th. A heavy artillery barrage was laid down when the German Second & Third with men advanced from the direction of GUISANCOURT FARM than they had on the previous day. It eventually all objectives were carried & the Battalion reinforced itself on the line which we consolidated on the previous day, looking up with the 13th Div. on to right. Throughout the operations on the 6th contact was maintained with the 50th Division. 2 Offs. killed 2nd wounded 10 missing, 2 died of wounds. Other ranks about 2,900 lowers. Two Cops of the R. Warwicks were attached to the Battalion & their place was taken two Companies of York's Regt. under Capt. W. S. Brown who were there under orders of the C.O.	
	7th Oct.	At 07.30 hours	the right flank of the Battalion was pushed	

WAR DIARY
INTELLIGENCE SUMMARY
(Erase heading not required.)

Army Form C. 2118.

Sheet 1.
1/7th The Sherwood Foresters.
11 pm

Place	Date	Hour	Summary of Events and Information	Remarks and references to Appendices
	7th		Forward about 200 yards and a line of posts established 1.N. of the Copse about 600 yards due East of GUISANCOURT FARM. GUISANCOURT FARM is about 2000 yds due South of the HINDENBURG LINE at RIDERS OUTREAUX and 2000yds E by N of the known posn of GOUAY. Casualties were 2/Lt Smith/Captain H.A. WATTS C Coy wounded by shell fire (leg) and 20 ORs wounded. About 2.30 hours the Battalion was relieved by the Leics & ND Division and moved to the neighbourhood of TORRENS CANAL on the GOUAY ESTREES road 1200 N.W. of ESTREES. The whole of the Brigade assembling in the neighbourhood and "B" Echelons joining their Battalions.	
	8th		0570 hours was the zero hour for afn attack by the South Africans The Brigade was in Corps Reserve and was ordered not to move after zero plus 2 hours. The whole of the morning was spent in re-fitting the Battalion and cleaning up generally, together with a careful enquiry as to collecting of stragglers.	

WAR DIARY
INTELLIGENCE SUMMARY.

Sept. 1/7th Bn. The Sherwood Foresters

Place	Date	Hour	Summary of Events and Information	Remarks and references to Appendices
October	6th Oct 18		Orders were received shortly before midnight for the Battalion to move at 0200 hours on Oct 6th Oct.	
			Lieut Col F.W. HALL MAYER M.C. rejoined the Battalion from Hospital (wounded 18.6.18. Italy) 2/Lt. N.C. GOODWIN & 2/Lt C.T. BOND joined the Battalion on first appointment.	
	9th		At 0200 hours the Battalion marched thro' BENEVOIR PUY CHAUX & thence along the main road towards NARETZ & the follow about 800 yards S.W. of SEPAIN FARM. Meanwhile the C.O. went to a conference with the Brigadier at PUYCHAUX & on his return here were barely time available for the issue of verbal orders for an attack. The general scheme of the attack was that the Battalion was to form the front line of the Brigade attacking on an initial frontage of approximately 1200 yds opening out to 1700 yds and the general objective which was 3400 yds from the "kick off". The 8th Bn the Notts and Derby supported in artillery formation	

WAR DIARY / INTELLIGENCE SUMMARY

Army Form C. 2118.

Sheet 9
11 Bn. The Sherwood Foresters

Place	Date	Hour	Summary of Events and Information	Remarks and references to Appendices

8 Oct 1918

Followed up the 13 D.L.I. in Reserve. The Brigade was ordered to deploy into attack formation on the N.E. edge of PREMONT. H.Q. Bn. went of the "Keep off" line and ran through LE TREU RIV SOLDATS (exclusive) on the South and RIBYE about 600 yds N of N. Officer's REU DE 4 VENIS & which was held by the 18 Warwicks, 50 Bde.

Two Coys had to be crossed at zero & two coys were 600 yds in rear. Had to be over this deep sunken lane. It ought to be remembered that the new Lagoust had a wide ones the sunken night & this made it difficult to give time & orders before zero hour. The final objective was the main road BAGNY – LE CATEAU between la riont de BAGNY (inclusive) and the road cross the railway (750 yds N.N.E. south of JONNECOURT). No opposition was encountered until the valley immediately West (200 & 600 yds) of the railway was reached. Here the battalion came under very heavy trench mortar M.G. fire

WAR DIARY
or
INTELLIGENCE SUMMARY.
(Erase heading not required.)

Army Form C. 2118.

Sheet 10

1/7 Bn. The Sherwood Foresters

Place	Date	Hour	Summary of Events and Information	Remarks and references to Appendices

October

From its left front 9 Flank moving to the Brigade on the left relieving Twenty villages in clearing MARETZ meanwhile the attackers on the right were being driven away by the movement carts operating on this Flank. Went back at 3 all worked with it day but the Engineers carriers worked on 9 carriages the Railway between LE TRON aux SOLDATS station the bridge over the Railway. Looking had been blown up we swung our advance slightly about 500 yds NE. Here they were afforded up by G York Light M.G. his company B.D.L Forward advance Right flank, but in so done the flanks turned up at w/o the advance on the original objective was adhered to. 9 York hung on the left. the 1/5 D.L.I. on the right the 9 Sherwoods They objective was reached reorganised by about 1600 hours advance on the success or zones our only reinforcements which had been very men were right from the flanks close of the Rickshaw was captured. A Batten Cavalry

WAR DIARY or INTELLIGENCE SUMMARY

Army Form C. 2118.

Sheet 11
1st Bn. The Hertford... Force Mas...

Place	Date	Hour	Summary of Events and Information	Remarks and references to Appendices
	8/10/18		Enter advanced on the further advance	
	9/10/18		Casualties Capt. C. W. BARTLETT M.C. killed by a shell whilst reconnoitring on the Battalion frontage on the main BUSIGNY- VIEUFLEAN Road. He was buried back of the vicinity in which he was brought to the H.Q. at 4/C. G. NUELS. 2/Lt. C. J. BOND wounded by shell G.O.C. Killed 1 - wounded 40 - missing - 3 - died of wounds	
	10		At 05.30 Enemy troops renewed the advance, 13 O.R-1. Enemy, 9 YORKS in support A 11 + 8 F. in reserve. The objective was the high ground N. & N.E. of ST. BENIN. It was no artillery barrage but I field artillery battery was occasionally employed to be attached to each Battalion, but unfortunately as art was available By 08.30 Enemy the Enemy Battalion commander Lieut. A.G. Jamieson the high ground N.E. of ST. BENIN - at this time still Bes... was not met until the 30 Division of Northumerion Army on	

Army Form C. 2118.

WAR DIARY
or
INTELLIGENCE SUMMARY.
(Erase heading not required.)

Sheet 17
1/4 Bn Monmouthshire

Place	Date	Hour	Summary of Events and Information	Remarks and references to Appendices
	27/4		the right the action having been held up by M.G. Snipers	
	10 am		Artillery support was brought to bear & a barrage opened the attack was continued at 11.40 hours the Battalions on the same order as in the morning, the battalion eventually retired to the reserve for the burying of the Regt. formed. Guarding the right flank, St Benin was captured by the two Companies leading Br Sahin. The enemy putting up slight opposition except in the nature of a heavy cross M.G. barrage. Two American Capt Crivelles reported to Co. for instructions and as they appeared to look to have for instructions they were attached to the battalion the second message I were expected to confirm with the 16 Welsh Regt keeping in close possible connection with the 20th Division divisions on right Casualties Capt Tolhurst & Lt Gibson are wounded only. Officer losses & O.Rs annulled.	
			Orders for the consolidation of the attack were captured	

WAR DIARY or INTELLIGENCE SUMMARY

Army Form C. 2118.

(Erase heading not required.)

Oct 13 1/4th Bn Manchester Lancs. R.

Place	Date	Hour	Summary of Events and Information	Remarks and references to Appendices
	Oct			
	11th		Orders of the C.R.E. of 4th Division were received at 0100 hours. Unit were carried shortly after their receipt by the Brigadier himself. Orders for the relief of the Royal Scots by the 2/4 Division were received. The Battalion not being itself relieved moved out about 1900 hours to HONNECHY, when the Brigade was concentrated. The Bn. casualties during the period Oct 4 to 10 inclusive were 3 Officers killed, 9 wounded (included 2/Lt J.R. PUCKEY attached) 2 wounded & duty, 1 died of wounds. O.R's 28 killed, 265 wounded, 26 missing of whom wounded O.R's to later. 53 wounded in hospitals were killed during the above operation as a result of a hostile bombing or distress.	
HONNECHY	12th		The Brigade marched from HONNECHY to PREMONT & went to billets.	
PREMONT	13th K		Reinforcement of 63 O.R's joined the Battalion. Extract from Battalion Routine Orders of Oct 13th:—	

Army Form C. 2118.

WAR DIARY
or
INTELLIGENCE SUMMARY.
(Erase heading not required.)

Sheet 14

Place	Date	Hour	Summary of Events and Information	Remarks and references to Appendices
Alfata	13		The commanding officer has much pleased on behalf of the Battalion to note the names which have been brought to his notice in connection with recent operations (Oct 5-10 ft.)	
			Major L.M. GIBSON. M.C.	
			Captain C.W. BARTLETT M.C. (killed in action)	
			" D.W. BIRD. M.C.	
			2/Lieut H.A. WATTS (wounded)	
			2/Lt R.J.N. SALTMAYER M.C.	
			Lt F.W.K. LAURIE. R.W.C	
			R.S.M.	
			26220 Col. Bow S.L.	
			16024 Sgt Sheekey A (M.M.)	
			62252 Lt. Pepel A.T.	
			622220 CSM Bate L	
			38082 Col Tolund L (M.M.)	
			16523 Col Maryhellor	

Army Form C. 2118.

WAR DIARY
or
INTELLIGENCE SUMMARY.
(Erase heading not required.)

Sheet 15.
1/1 Bn Sherwood Foresters

Place	Date	Hour	Summary of Events and Information	Remarks and references to Appendices
Etrun	13 Sept		List of names (contd)	
			241608 - Pte Shillard W. 11668 - Pte Garner E.	
			306/224 - Pte Storey S.H. 42305 - Pte Betts W.H.	
			6111937 - Pte Hall A. 42305 - Pte Scott A.	
			16376 - Pte Page J. 241611 - Pte Goode A.	
			43390 - Pte Forrest G. 241116 - Pte Elliers G.H.	
			107748 - Pte Pollard R.W. 19463 - Pte Heath F.	
			16147 - Pte Cordy P. 235.9 - Pte Webster E.	
			218445 - Pte Withers E. 16076 - Pte Fewkes L.	
			2525 - Pte Turner A. 4668 - " Glew J.	
			16922 - " Teague R.a. 42203 - " Merrin F.	
			19258 - " Smith J. 14809 - " Trevoroth a.	
			12947 - " Escott J. 17606 Sgt Oxley L.	
			6786 - Sgt Burry J. 19339 - " Litwell H.	
			7303 Pte Foot G.W. 276.H.K. Mallick G. (m.m.)	
			269801 - Pte Hill E. 26620 - Maker H.	

Army Form C. 2118.

WAR DIARY
or
INTELLIGENCE SUMMARY.

(Erase heading not required.)

Sheet 16

11 Bn the Cheshire Regiment

Instructions regarding War Diaries and Intelligence Summaries are contained in F. S. Regs., Part II. and the Staff Manual respectively. Title pages will be prepared in manuscript.

Place	Date	Hour	Summary of Events and Information	Remarks and references to Appendices
PREMONT	Oct 14		Lieut C.R. OXFORD takes over pay & duties of "B" Coy with effect from 10th October 1918.	
	13		10 Drums of PREMONT During the last two days the Batln has re-organised & re-equipped itself. Coys & min Littees.	
PREMONT	16		Lieut E.C. CLEEVE (Manchester Regt) joined the Batln as Transport Officer.	
	17		Batln left PREMONT for MARETZ. Genl E CLEEVE admitted to hospital.	
	18		Batln left MARETZ for HONNECHY.	
	19		HONNECHY	
	20		HONNECHY	
	21		HONNECHY. Enemy aircraft showered lights incendiary by Brigade runners signallers & others Roll no 7 sheet 1 OR killed & OR's wounded of this Batln.	

Army Form C. 2118.

WAR DIARY
or
INTELLIGENCE SUMMARY.
(Erase heading not required.)

Sheet 17
of War Diary of ....

Place	Date	Hour	Summary of Events and Information	Remarks and references to Appendices
	6/1 10 Oct		attached to Brigade for [?] of the [?] was [?] on [?] but our guns ever well except guards where is every reason to believe that to an [?] owing to hazy [?]	
[?]	22nd		at dawn Lieut A.D. PARKIN M.C. joined the Battalion. The following officers of the Oxford T.B.L.1 joined the Battalion. 2/Lt G. TARRIS, 2/Lt H. NEWMAN, 2/Lt [?] MMINGS, 2/Lt PEARD, 2/Lt TODD, R.L. COVINGTON & S. AUSTIN from the M.G.C.	
	23rd		Orders having been received the Battalion fell in [?] at [?] [?] & proceeded to take up [?] E of LE CATEAU & to be attacked by the Brigade on [?] AT LE CATEAU. The Battalion [?] its last [?] [?] the [?] the Battalion [?] its last [?] [?] the [?] LE CATEAU there was little difficulty but in reinforced the [?] of the [?] Battery, the artillery barrage being [?] beyond LE CATEAU, when the Brigade served [?] forward they were a barrage for [?] infantry to [?] which was to take place E of LE CATEAU.	

WAR DIARY
or
INTELLIGENCE SUMMARY.
(Erase heading not required.)

Army Form C. 2118.

Place	Date	Hour	Summary of Events and Information	Remarks and references to Appendices

BASUEL. Bn. the Battalion was carrying up the recesses - front road and was telephoned by the 3rd Bn. in front side in two own held up by the Brigade what was to take the first I second of Baisieux. Seeing the second of evacuating the same in heavy shell fire every - a good number of casualties occurred. The Battalion dug in a left bank until ?? of the road.

At in the morning the Battalion moved from LE CATEAU sea DENNERUE and moved through the GUT Brigade until the bomb of the Brigade deployed up a back formation. D'Forks kept on the right B.P.'s in the timber of W'S.L. an the left.

For a time running heavy bus l'Eveque the Brigade due ... the night 2nd Lt J PICKARD who was along 20 ??? ??? with the Brigade on our left was wounded.

Killed 18
W. Munroe Lowlie

Army Form C. 2118.

WAR DIARY
or
INTELLIGENCE SUMMARY.
(Erase heading not required.)

Instructions regarding War Diaries and Intelligence Summaries are contained in F. S. Regs., Part II. and the Staff Manual respectively. Title pages will be prepared in manuscript.

Sheet 19

1/1th Bn. The Sherwood Foresters

Place	Date	Hour	Summary of Events and Information	Remarks and references to Appendices
	Sep 6		At 11.30 a.m. the Brigade moved forward the route on the previous day. A halt was made near the crossing on the River Somme, which was not provided. Upon entering the standing corn heavy rifle fire was encountered. Shortly after, it was commenced & the Battalion came across a line of trenches made & when advancing through this being enemy sniper fire caused most of the casualties incurred in this fighting. B 2 Coy forced the front line & took up position in & Coys on Ridge & Lewis guns and a good force on the ridge leading to Fontaine au Bois on the right of our sector, along with a few Coys from return of the 13th D.I. succeeded in silencing the enemy machine guns & rifles. After this the advance was renewed without much opposition but under heavy infantry fire. Eventually we arrived at Fontaine au Bois, quickly made. Immediately on arrival two Lewis guns (1 B Coy) was on duty & field guns were open upon	

(3017S) Wt W3158/P56. 60,000 12/17. D. D. & L. Sch. 52a. Forms/C2118/15.

WAR DIARY
or
INTELLIGENCE SUMMARY.
(Erase heading not required.)

Army Form C. 2118.

Place: In the Bivouac Area

Date	Hour	Summary of Events and Information	Remarks and references to Appendices
Oct 20		The 1st Royal Warwicks having moved through to further objective the village was then carefully searched & filled up by No 1 Coy. An enemy field gun was established 100 yds East of the LANDRECIES–BOUSIES road about No 1 Coy's dug in posn SE of Rd LE CATEAU–FONTAINE AU BOIS road. Orders were received for us to dig in not further than 1400 hours & from up with the Warwicks. This manner we eventually accomplished without any slight enemy machine gun artillery reply having some few casualties in the effort. The Brigade pushed in and were relieved during the evening by the Cheshire Regt & marched back to position required. The previous night prior to this action casualties – Capt. J H SPEAR M.C. wounded, Capt N A CLIFTON M.C. wounded at duty, Lieut H D PARKIN M.C. shot over command 1 No 2 Coy, 2nd Lt T M TOMKINS & Lieut W D LEES F STUBBINGTON joined Battalion	

Army Form C. 2118.

WAR DIARY
or
INTELLIGENCE SUMMARY.
(Erase heading not required.)

Instructions regarding War Diaries and Intelligence Summaries are contained in F. S. Regs., Part II. and the Staff Manual respectively. Title pages will be prepared in manuscript.

Place	Date	Hour	Summary of Events and Information	Remarks and references to Appendices
	Oct 25		The Battalion moved forward into FONTAINE AU BOIS not	
			without some opposition. Lt. Col. B.D.L.S. of 4/K.R.R.C.	
			was killed.	
			FONTAINE AU BOIS was shelled by B heavy guns.	
			Had rather an unpleasant time in Château.	
	26		Château B.W.BIRD M.C. wounded.	see appendices
			Captain B.W.BIRD M.C. wounded.	
			FONTAINE AU BOIS	
	27		FONTAINE AU BOIS. Very light shelling by enemy.	
			2/Lt R.L.T.M. SALTMAYER M.C. proceeded on leave to U.K.	
			FONTAINE AU BOIS. Lieut. W.W. LEE struck off strength of Bn of 7th L.T.M.B.	
	28		Battalion out. Then marching into Lieut. W.R. COWAN M.C. Buffs joined & assumed	
			at 9.00 hours to take command of the Bn again.	
	29		The 13 K.R.R. L. a doubtful to such known their Bn for	
			were successful in inflicting casualties on enemy without	
			losses to Battalion and ordered to take them close as possible	

Instructions regarding War Diaries and Intelligence Summaries are contained in F. S. Regs., Part II, and the Staff Manual respectively. Title pages will be prepared in manuscript.

WAR DIARY
or
~~INTELLIGENCE SUMMARY.~~

(*Erase heading not required.*)

Army Form C. 2118.

October — Sheet 22 — 11 Bn Sherwood Foresters

Place	Date	Hour	Summary of Events and Information	Remarks and references to Appendices
	Oct 29th		the 9th Yorks Regt being on the right. The relief was effected without molestation, No 2 Coy on the right, No 2 Coy on the left with platoons from each Coy in support.	
	30th		Front line comparatively quiet. During the night the support line & to the rear of it & the village were shelled at intervals.	
			Lieut A McKECHIE (attached 9 YORKS Regt) Special Leave to U.K. T.M.B brought into action during the evening against enemy M.G. Posts.	
	Oct 31st		In the early hours the support line & village were shelled, a good proportion of gas shells being used. The Battalion was relieved by the 1/8 Royal Warwicks without attracting any fire from the enemy. Battalion moved into Billets at POMMERAL via MALGAMI. — Reinforcements 84 O.Rs. Casualties from 23rd Oct to 31st Oct: ORs 22 Killed 89 wounded 14 missing 3 Died of wounds. (Details of officer casualties are given upon the dates they occurred)	

W R Corrall Lieut Colonel
Commdg 11th (S) Battalion
The Sherwood Foresters

(A9175) Wt W2358/P360 600,000 12/17 D. D. & L. Sch. 52a. Forms/C2118/15.

12a

"Addenda"

Oct 25. At 1700 hours Lt. Col. H.N. YOUNG, DSO, C.O. of the Battalion was killed by shell fire, the Adjutant Capt. B.W. BIRD M.C. wounded, whilst coming to his new H.Q. in FONTAINE AU BOIS, along the POMMERUIL - FONTAINE AU BOIS road (57 BNE) L16a. Death was instantaneous, his body was brought back to POMMERUIL.

Oct 26. The late Lt. Col. H.N. YOUNG, DSO was buried today in the cemetery at POMMERUIL.

Sheet
11 North Staff[?]
Army Form C. 2118.

WAR DIARY
INTELLIGENCE SUMMARY.
(Erase heading not required.)

Instructions regarding War Diaries and Intelligence Summaries are contained in F. S. Regs., Part II. and the Staff Manual respectively. Title pages will be prepared in manuscript.

Place	Date	Hour	Summary of Events and Information	Remarks and references to Appendices
POMMERUIL	1918 Nov 1		Battalion engaged in finding reinforcements, reorganisation & re-fitting.	
POMMERUIL	Nov 2	0630 / 1000	The Battalion marched to the Battle at LE CATEAU, afterwards moving on ST BENIN. The cookers were taken & dinners were served there.	
		1500	The Battalion watched an exhibition of bridge building across the river at ST BENIN by the 18" WORCESTERS. People were largely used in the exhibition. The Battalion afterwards marched back to POMMERUIL.	
			In the evening the C.O. entertained the officers of the Battalion to dinner.	
POMMERUIL Nov 3			The following officers joined the Battalion upon first appointment: 2nd Lieut. R.P.PRATT, J.D.WALL, J.MORRALL, J.A.BURNS, R.BAILEY, R.P.STEPHENSON, V.L.ROWE, L.J.GOOSENS.	1. 38
POMMERUIL			The C.O. along with the Company Commanders went to MALGARNI to reconnoitre position for a starting point on the 4th inst.	

Sheet 2

Army Form C. 2118.

WAR DIARY
INTELLIGENCE SUMMARY
(Erase heading not required.)

Instructions regarding War Diaries and Intelligence Summaries are contained in F. S. Regs., Part II, and the Staff Manual respectively. Title pages will be prepared in manuscript.

Place	Date	Hour	Summary of Events and Information	Remarks and references to Appendices
POMMERUIL	1918 Nov 4	03.45	The Battalion moved off from POMMERUIL at zero minus 2 hours - 03.45 to MALGARNI, where they lay in on the selected positions. The Brigade's objective was a line running S.E. of the RIVER SAMBRE (B>7a) 6 — them on the LANDRECIES - MARBILLES Road, the attacking formation being 9" YORKS REGT on the left, the 11" SHERWOOD FORESTERS on the right from RUE DES JUIFS & RUE DE MARAIS, with the 13" D.L.I in support. The objective of the 75" Brigade was a line running East of LANDRECIES. & being artillery barrage was put down and in places the enemy made a vigorous reply. After the barrage lifted the Battalion moved across the fields to the chemin on the LE FAUX - LANDRECIES Road, about 600 yards, where they took up relay the race for about 600 yards, where they took up positions in the fields at right angles to the road as follows	Start ARM

Sheet 3

WAR DIARY
INTELLIGENCE SUMMARY
(Erase heading not required.)

Army Form C. 2118.

Place	Date	Hour	Summary of Events and Information	Remarks and references to Appendices

"A" Coy in front, B Coy in support, C Coy in reserve. When the 75th Brigade had taken their objective, the Battalion passed through them to the East of LANDRECIES. A Coy although meeting with a considerable amount of M.G. & rifle fire, succeeded in taking up a position on the Western bank of the stream running by ST. ROCH HOSPICE with their right on the Northern side of the LANDRECIES-MAROILLES Road. This Company captured two 4.2 guns, one field gun & 3 prisoners.

B Coy also succeeded in taking up their allotted position on the Southern side of the LANDRECIES-MAROILLES Road, through (G.30.a.7.8, G.19.c.7.6 although harassed by enemy M.G. rifle fire from their right flank. This Company captured 1 Officer, 21 O.Rs, 1 Browning gun & 1 Anti-tank rifle.

C Coy in support (G.23.c.1.1) was practically ourselves. Although the 2 bridges had been blown up, the Engineers had got sufficient plank & [indecipherable] (peaks, tires?) [illegible] across the [stream?] and the

WAR DIARY
INTELLIGENCE SUMMARY

Army Form C. 2118.
Sheet 4

Place	Date	Hour	Summary of Events and Information	Remarks and references to Appendices
	1918 Nov		cont. to enable the Battalion to make the crossings quickly.	
		17.30	The three Companies concentrated at 17.30 hours at the road junction G30.a.9.8, there was a strong place a large mine blown up just in front. 'A' Coy meeting a large crater in the centre of the road, but happily did not cause any casualties. 'A' Coy pushed out supports along the LANDRECIES - MAROILLES Road at a distance of 1400 yards from the road junction. B Coy pushed out and along the road to BOUTLETTE FARM. C Company being later on the right flank. Lieuts SAULE BRYANTE & Buckingham were brought up a further the flank's on the left flank 'A' Coy were in close touch with the 9" YORKS Regt., the 13" D.L.I. being in support. The outpost line ran from G.30 central along H.25 central, H.25.b.2.6 H.19.a.x.y. Patrols were sent out & a number of enemy were killed taken back from the farm buildings. 3 Prisoners were taken during the night.	Appx B & W

(49173) Wt W335/P361 6,000 12/17 D.D.& L. Sch. 52a. Forms/C2118/13

Army Form C. 2118.
Sheet 5

WAR DIARY
or
INTELLIGENCE SUMMARY.
(Erase heading not required.)

Instructions regarding War Diaries and Intelligence Summaries are contained in F. S. Regs., Part II. and the Staff Manual respectively. Title pages will be prepared in manuscript.

Place	Date	Hour	Summary of Events and Information	Remarks and references to Appendices
FAIR DE FRANCE	Nov 4 1918		Casualties. Offr Killed 2nd Lieut R M HALE & H NEEBLE joined the Battalion	
	Nov 5 06.15		The Battalion moved forward at 06.15 hours the Van Guard being formed with the Class "B" Officers accompany under command of 2nd Lieutenant 12th LANCERS, 1 Section 130th Field Coy R.E. & 11th SHERWOOD FORESTERS, A Battery, 110th Brigade R F A. R Coy formed the Van Guard, the remainder forming the Main Guard. Main Body 9th YORKS REGT, 13/74L, "A" Company 25th Bn M GUN CORPS, 130th Field Coy R E (Less 1 section) x 110th Brigade R F A. The route was LE PRESAU - LA BLANCHISSERIE - CATILLON FARM. OLD MILL DES PRES - RUE DE JULES & MAROILLES. The Van Guard encountered heavy MG & rifle fire from the high ground in A.14 but succeeded in getting on O.L.D MILL DES PRES. Good work was made throughout the day of the Cavalry who formed themselves to be of great assistance both for scouting & the quick conveyance of messages. The bridge at OLD MILL DES PRES. having been blown up the Battalion waited	57.A 57.A N.W

WAR DIARY
INTELLIGENCE SUMMARY
(Erase heading not required.)

Army Form C. 2118.

Sheet 6

Place: [blank]
Date: 1918 Nov 5
Hour: [blank]

Summary of Events and Information:

through the stream. A Coy & platoon of B Coy were sent forward to mop up MAROILLES and B Coy & the remaining platoons to give support. The leaving Company advancing rapidly and opposition pushed rapidly forward through MAROILLES and prevented the enemy blowing up any of the bridges over the river. This Company (A Coy & Platoon of B Coy) dug in & pushed forward & established outpost positions from H.17.c.7.9 to H.11.a.8.5. Some heavy M.G. inflicted mortar fire was met with but being reinforced by B Coy & Platoon of C Coy the position was gained and consolidated on Ration Farm — J.1. Coy they were close support. The offensive was chiefly from the high ground in H.12.a. The enemy made a good attempt to clear the ground, but the above moving of the enemy was against them. The artillery concentrated on this area, but there were no appreciable casualties by the fire would be at night, and was established until the 9 YORKS left on our left.

Remarks and references to Appendices: [blank]

Army Form C. 2118.

Sheet 1

WAR DIARY

INTELLIGENCE SUMMARY.
(Erase heading not required.)

Instructions regarding War Diaries and Intelligence Summaries are contained in F.S. Regs., Part II. and the Staff Manual respectively. Title pages will be prepared in manuscript.

Place	Date	Hour	Summary of Events and Information	Remarks and references to Appendices
MAROILLES	1918 Nov 5		After leaving LE PRESAU, several batteries of artillery were seen retained by the Battalion. There were 600-700 yards in front of the 9th YORKS. Regt outpost line, who had the task with which the enemy had left his positions on the right of the 4th Corps. Casualties — 2nd Lieut. L. J. GOOSENS wounded. O.R. 1 Killed 25 Wounded — Honey 1 Died of Wounds.	
MAROILLES	Nov 6		The advance was ordered to be continued on the Brigade front. 74th Infantry Brigade on the Right, 7th Infantry Brigade on the Left. The 9 YORKS. Regt taking the place of the 11 SHERWOOD FORESTERS on the advance Guard. This Battalion to follow the 13 DLI in the Rear Bay. The Van Guard forced through the outpost line at 0700 hours, when the Battalion formed up on H.17 b.5.1.7 - H.17 R.38. About then advanced shelled the main road from the CEMETERY to MAROILLES, the Battalion were therefore pushed forward along the ride road through H.17 a.9.7 - H.18 a.2.5. leaving only one / on each light casualties 2/Lt F.W. TOMPKINS wounded, OR 4 wounded	was not SYA Nov

WAR DIARY
INTELLIGENCE SUMMARY

Army Form C. 2118.

Sheet 8

Place	Date	Hour	Summary of Events and Information	Remarks and references to Appendices
	1918 Nov 6		1 hussy armoured cars, as well as the Cavalry assisted the 9 YORKS Regt in the advance which however was held up when nearing MARBAIX. At 17.00 6/13.15 two an artillery barrage was put down after which the advance proceeded & after a running fight in MARBAIX the 9 YORKS Regt obtained possession of the village to the South an outpost line on the East of it. The Battalion moved forward and took over part of the outpost line from the YORKS Regt after the arrival of the Battalion in MARBAIX the village was shelled for about an hour tolerably without causing any casualties. Towards over night the enemy's fire died down considerably. Machine guns also assisted in holding the line, plenty amm established with the 13 DLI on our Left Flank.	
MARBAIX No 70800			At 08.00 hours the 75 Brigade passed through the 74 Brigade and the Battalion went into billets.	

Army Form C. 2118.

Sheet 7

WAR DIARY
INTELLIGENCE SUMMARY.
(Erase heading not required.)

Place	Date	Hour	Summary of Events and Information	Remarks and references to Appendices
MARBAIX	1918 Nov 7	15:40	Orders were received at 14:30 hours for the Battalion to move to MAROILLES, passing the starting point at 15:45 hours.	
MAROILLES			Upon arrival at MAROILLES the Battalion went into billets. It showed no indication that the enemy had been opposed to them town on the 5th & 6th inst.	
	No Stop		Orders were received at 01:30 hours for the Battalion to move to BOUSIES, passing the starting point at 04:45 hours. The Battalion marched through LANDRECIES & BOUSIES into billets. The total expenditure for the operations from November the 4th-7th were remarkably light being under 50.	
BOUSIES			Re organisation of Battalion.	
	10	11:00	Church Parade. 2/Lieut F.W.TOMKINS rejoined the Battalion. A/Major L.H.GIBSON M.C & Lt W.A.WILSON on leave to U.K. Battalion cleared all made gates around BOUSIES. Capt O.R.ORCHARD on leave to U.K.	
	11	11:00	An armoured car arrived in BOUSIES at 10:30 hours warning to all Divisions that the armistice was to be signed and hostilities would cease at 11:00 hours from today.	

Army Form C. 2118.
Sheet 10

WAR DIARY
or
INTELLIGENCE SUMMARY.
(Erase heading not required.)

Instructions regarding War Diaries and Intelligence Summaries are contained in F. S. Regs., Part II. and the Staff Manual respectively. Title pages will be prepared in manuscript.

Place	Date	Hour	Summary of Events and Information	Remarks and references to Appendices
BOUSIES	1918 Nov 11		Battalion training as per programme.	
"	12		Battalion training as per programme.	
			The Commanding Officer has much pleasure in publishing the following list of names which have been brought to his notice in connection with recent operations (October 23rd to 31st inclusive)	
			A/Capt. W.A.CLIFTON. M.C.	
			T/Capt. F.W.K.LAWRIE.	
			305049 S.C. G.A.JOHNSON.	
			920810 Pte J WALMSLEY	
			118238 J.J.WARDLE	
			268955 L/Cpl F.C.FRISBY	
			71786 Pte J.N.BLOW	
			53960 Sgt S.B.RICHARDSON	
			58534 Pte G.NICHOLSON	
			203193 A/Cpl H.T.CHAPPIN	
			19928 Pte I.SMITH	
			73189 Sgt. J.R.GARFOOT	
			2/Lieut C.H.ROSE on leave to U.K.	
			The Regimental Band arranged for the HQ Mess	

(49175) Wt W3348/P560 600,000 12/7 D.D.&L. Sch. 52a. Forms/C.2118/13.

Army Form C. 2118.

Sheet 11

WAR DIARY
INTELLIGENCE SUMMARY.
(Erase heading not required.)

Place	Date	Hour	Summary of Events and Information	Remarks and references to Appendices
BOUSIES	1918 Nr.13		At 10.49 hours the Battalion marched from BOUSIES	
LE CATEAU			via FORÊT - MONTAY to LE CATEAU into Billets.	
			A/Capt W.A. CLIFTON on leave to U.K.	
			2/Lieut GWIMBER rejoined the Battalion from ITALY	
			Lieut Illy rejoined Battalion from hospital	
LE CATEAU Nr.14	-13		Lieut J. R. J'nner Battalion from hospital	
LE CATEAU	-15		Lee/Lieut. S.P. HOWELL reported him arrived on first	
			appointment and taken on strength of Battalion	
			2/Lt Tho. rejoined Battalion from hospital	
			Major L.R. HALFORD, M.C. returned from the establishment	
			of the Battalion with effect from 23.9.18 Auth MS/P/8066 dated 9/11/18	
			Battalion engaged in ordinary parades.	
LE CATEAU Nr.16			Standard inspected by the Commanding Officer and O.C.	
			25th Divisional Band at 11.00 hours	
LE CATEAU Nr.17			Interior Economy except Company arrangements	
			Voluntary Church Services	

WAR DIARY
INTELLIGENCE SUMMARY

Army Form C. 2118.
Sheet 12.

Place	Date	Hour	Summary of Events and Information	Remarks and references to Appendices
LE CATEAU	18/Nov	10.00	Board assembled to check Mobile Reserve stores and ammunition. Medical inspection of all the Battalion. Ordinary training. Lieut. A.D. PARKIN, M.C. took over command of "D" Coy. from 17-11-18. 2nd Lieut. C.L.J.M. SALLMAYER, N.C. rejoins from leave to U.K. 2nd Lieut. T. HODSON rejoins from Adjutants Course Cambridge. Lt. Col. R.B. CORRAH N.C. reported wounded (gas) on duty. 30.10.18. Extract from London Gazette dated 15.11.18. Temp. 2nd Lt. (Acting Captain) M.A. CLIFTON, M.C. to be Temp. Captain. (16 June) Temp. Lieut. (Adg. Capt. Retd.) J.M. SPICER, M.C. to be Temp. Captain. (10 Sept.) Appointments — 2nd/Lt. F.C. SMITH to be Actg. Adjutant 26 Oct. to 13th Nov. 1918. Capt. I.M. MARSH, M.C. to be Acting Adjutant 14th Nov. 1918. 2nd Lt. F.C. SMITH to be Assistant Adjutant 14. Nov. 1918. Battalion route march.	
LE CATEAU	19/Nov		Two Companies engaged on salvage work. Two Coys carried on ordinary training.	
LE CATEAU	20/Nov		Lt. & Rev'd L.A. BIRLEY taken on strength of the Battalion.	

Sheet 13.

Army Form C. 2118.

WAR DIARY
or
INTELLIGENCE SUMMARY.
(Erase heading not required.)

Place	Date	Hour	Summary of Events and Information	Remarks and references to Appendices
	1918			
LE CATEAU	21/11		Capt. F.W.K. LAWRIE, R.A.M.C. proceeded to England for demobilization and attached to Battalion strength of the Battalion. Two Companies on Salvage work. One Coy. at the Baths.	
LE CATEAU	22/11		Boxing Classes started. Capt. H.R. OLIVER, N.C., C.A.M.C. joined Battalion as Medical Officer. 2nd. LIEUT. R. BAILEY admitted to hospital, sick. Two Coys on Salvage work, one Coy at the Baths. A Choir was formed to assist at the Church Services held by the Battalion.	
LE CATEAU	23/11		LIEUT. (R.M.) F. LIDSTONE, D.C.M. proceeded to the Base and to strike off the strength of the Battalion 23.11.18. 2nd. LIEUT. N.C. GODWIN is appointed Acting Quartermaster 23.11.18.	
LE CATEAU	24/11		Divine Service. 2nd. LIEUT. R.L. COWISTON appointed Educational Officer for the Battalion. Coys. on Salvage work.	
LE CATEAU	25/11		Revd. A. MURCHIE rejoined from leave to the United Kingdom 25/11.	

Army Form C. 2118.
Sheet 14.

WAR DIARY
or
INTELLIGENCE SUMMARY.
(Erase heading not required.)

Instructions regarding War Diaries and Intelligence Summaries are contained in F.S. Regs., Part II. and the Staff Manual respectively. Title pages will be prepared in manuscript.

Place	Date	Hour	Summary of Events and Information	Remarks and references to Appendices
LE CATEAU	Nov 25		Lieut. E.C. CLEEVE rejoined from hospital	
LE CATEAU	Nov 26		Two Coys. on salvage work, two Coys training. Voluntary work. Lieut. H. MOORE M.C. joined Battalion 26.11.18.	
LE CATEAU	Nov 27		Salvage. A football match was played in the afternoon between A.& B. Coys. & the XIIIth Corps Competition, resulting in a draw of two goals each. In the evening a Battalion Concert was held. A/Capt. G.N. GIMBER accidentally wounded (at duty). Major L.H. GIBSON M.C. rejoined from leave to U.K. 27.11.18. 2nd Lieut. N.A. WILSON rejoined from leave to U.K. 28.11.18. The following awards have been made by H.M. The King of Italy. To A/Major L.H. GIBSON M.C. The CROCE DI GUERRA. 11359 C.S.M. S. THOMPSON. The CROCE DI GUERRA.	
LE CATEAU	Nov 29		Lieut. Col. N.R. CORRALL N.C. granted leave to U.K. M/Capt. O.T. ORCHARD rejoined from leave to U.K. Battalion moved by March Route to ST. HILLAIRE.	

Army Form C. 2118.

Sheet 15.

WAR DIARY
or
INTELLIGENCE SUMMARY.
(Erase heading not required.)

Instructions regarding War Diaries and Intelligence Summaries are contained in F. S. Regs., Part II, and the Staff Manual respectively. Title pages will be prepared in manuscript.

Place	Date	Hour	Summary of Events and Information	Remarks and references to Appendices
ST. HILLAIRE	Nov 24		The following awards have been made authority handed by His Majesty the King.	
			D.C.M. to 1916 Sgt. W.H.COLLINS.	
			M.M. to 6920 98 Pte. WALMSLEY.J., 200895 Pte. FRISBY.F.C.	
			53960 Sgt. RICHARDSON.S.B., 203193 L/Cpl. CHAPPIN.H.	
			40538 Pte. WATTS.F., 36100 Pte. STALLEBRASS.A.	
			118230 Pte. WARDLE.J.T., 41786 Pte. BLOW.J.N.	
			58534 Pte. NICHOLSON.G., 43015 Pte. SMITH.I.	
			260625 Pte. PERCIVAL.H., 108407 Pte. DUNGAN.G.A.	
			73199 Pte. SUTHERLAND.J.A.	
			Bar to M.C. to	
			Capt. B.W.BIRD M.C.	
			2nd Lt. (A/Lt.) I.M.SALLMAYER M.C.	
ST.HILLAIRE Nov 30			M.C. to	
			2nd Lt. (A/Capt.) H.A. WATTS.	

B.W.Bithern Major
Commanding 1/1to Sherwood Foresters

11 N&D Section
Army Form C. 2118.
Vol 3

WAR DIARY or INTELLIGENCE SUMMARY

1st Sheet.

(Erase heading not required.)

Place	Date 1918	Hour	Summary of Events and Information	Remarks and references to Appendices
ST.HILAIRE	1 Dec	11.00	Voluntary Church Service.	
Do.	2 Dec		Two Coys. engaged in Salvage work, two on Ordinary training.	
Do.	3 Dec		Two Coys. engaged in Salvage work, two in Ordinary training.	
ST.HILAIRE	4 Dec	11.30	Lecture by Col. Dowling on "Reinstatement Problems".	
			Under authority Amdts. by H.M. the King of Italy, the following award has been made to 17957 Sgt. H.E. ANTCLIFFE, D.C.M., M.M. "The Italian medal for Valour (bronze)" His Majesty King George V. and the H.R.H. The Prince of Wales walked	
		15.00	through the village of ST.HILAIRE.	
			2nd Lieut. O.R. ORCHARD appointed Acting Captain whilst commanding a Company 26th Oct. 1918. (Authy. M.S.Lst No. 215 dated 21/4/18.)	
ST.HILAIRE	5 Dec		Salvage operations by two Coys. Training by two Coys.	3
		14.30	Lecture by Professor A.C.D. CROMMELIN on Astronomy.	39
ST.HILAIRE	6 Dec		Lecture to A.&B. Coys. by Education Officer. Two Coys. on salvage.	
			Capt. F.H. ERITH rejoined Battalion on 6.12.18 and Taken on strength.	
			Capt. B.W. BIR. R.A.M.C. (previously reported as missing) now also reported 24.11.18	
ST.HILAIRE	7 Dec		Battalion at the Baths.	

WAR DIARY or INTELLIGENCE SUMMARY

Army Form C. 2118.

2nd [Regt].

Place	Date	Hour	Summary of Events and Information	Remarks and references to Appendices
ST.HILAIRE	1.12.18		Presentation parade address to the following by the G.O.C. 2 Sth. Divn.	
			19958 Pte. J. SMITH. — Military Medal. 17854 Pte. A. AINSWORTH - Military Medal	
			305490 Sgt. G. MYKES - Military Medal. 16565 Cpl. A. HARNER - Military Medal	
ST.HILAIRE	8 Dec	10.00	Voluntary Church Parade	
		14.00	Football match in XIII th Corps Competition 'B' Coy. v 'D' Coy. Result draw.	
			One goal all.	
ST.HILAIRE	9 Dec		Salvage operations continued by two Coys. Two Coys Interior Economy.	
			Presentation of medal ribbons to the following:—	
			2nd Lieut. C.L.J.M. SALLMAYER. M.C. — Bar to M.C.	
			1916 Sgt. W. COLLINS. — D.C.M.	
			118230 Pte. T.J. WARDLE — Military Medal. 71786 Pte. J.N. BLOW - Military Medal	
			730015 Pte. I. SMITH — Military Medal. 73199 Pte. J.A. SUTHERLAND - Military Medal	
			23376 Pte. G. SPRUCE — Military Medal. 92098 Pte. J. WALMSLEY. — Military Medal.	
		14.30	Lecture by Capt. Alston R.A.F. on "Flying".	
ST.HILAIRE	10 Dec		Salvage operations continued by two Coys. Two Coys. training.	
			2nd Lt. B.W. JAMES and Sec. Lt. C.R. JARVIS reported arrival and taken on strength	

WAR DIARY
INTELLIGENCE SUMMARY
(Erase heading not required.)

3rd sheet.

Army Form C. 2118.

Place	Date	Hour	Summary of Events and Information	Remarks and references to Appendices
ST. HILAIRE	11 Dec		Salvage operations continued	JMR
	12 Dec		Salvage operations continued	JMR
			Lieut V.G.P. BROUGH proceeded on a course on "Organised Revolution"	JMR
			Promotions	
			Extract from Gazette d. 6/12/18.	JMR
			Temporary Major G.N. GIMBER to be Temp'y Lieut. 26 Oct 1918.	
			Extract from Gazette d. 9/12/18.	JMR
			Temp'y 2nd Lt T. HODSON to be Temp'y Lieut 26 Oct 1918 (no remuneration)	
			Relinq Temp. G.N. GIMBER.	JMR
ST. HILAIRE	13 Dec		Salvage operations continued.	JMR
	14 Dec		Salvage operations continued.	JMR
		4.00	Football Match "B" Coy. v "D" Coy. Result "B" Coy 2 — "B" Coy 1.	JMR
			"B" Coy represent the Bn. in the Corps Competition.	JMR
ST. HILAIRE	15 Dec	10.30	Voluntary Church Service.	JMR
		4.00	Bn. plays "D" Batt. 110 R.F.A. at football. Result one goal all.	JMR
ST. HILAIRE	16 Dec		Salvage operations continued.	JMR

WAR DIARY

Army Form C. 2118.

INTELLIGENCE SUMMARY. 4th Bn.

Place	Date	Hour	Summary of Events and Information	Remarks and references to Appendices
ST. HILAIRE	17th		Salvage Operations Continued.	
			Capt. T.A. COTTER M.C., C.F. proceeded to England on expiration of Contract.	
			100 miners proceeded to England and struck off strength	
			Capt. H.G. OLIVER M.C. R.A.M.C. proceed to U.K. on leave.	
			Appendices Communiques, etc.	
			Extracts from M.S. List No. 217 dated 8/12/18.	
			Notts. & Derby Rgt.	
			11th Bn. — Capt. C.E. HUDSON, V.C., D.S.O., M.C., Notts. & Derby Rgt. relinquishes the Temp. rank of Lt. Col. on ceasing to Command Bn. (to Command 2nd Bn.) 29th September 1918.	
			Temp. Major (Acting Lt. Col.) W.R. CORRALL, M.C., C.G. Regt., Capt. E. Kent Rgt.) to Command Bn. and to be Temp. Lt. Col. to fill establishment 29th October 1918.	
	18th Dec		Salvage Operations Continued.	
	19th		Salvage Operations Continued.	

WAR DIARY
or
INTELLIGENCE SUMMARY.
(Erase heading not required.)

Army Form C. 2118.

5th Sheet.

Place	Date	Hour	Summary of Events and Information	Remarks and references to Appendices
ST HILAIRE	19/8		The Battn had baths at AVESNES LES AUBERT — 2 COMPANIES.	9.h.h.
	20th Decr		The undermentioned were awarded decorations as shown.	10.h.h.
			T/2°Lt (A/Capt) W A CLIFTON. M.C. — Bar to the Military Cross.	10.h.h.
			T/Captain F W R LAWRIE RAMC — Military Cross	10.h.h.
			305649 Sgt G. A. JOHNSON — D.C.M.	10.h.h.
			43189 Sgt J R GARFOOT — D.C.M	
	21st Decr		The Battn had baths at AVESNES LES AUBERT — 2 COMPANIES.	10.h.h.
			T/Lieut T. HODSON is appointed Assistant Adjutant from date.	10.h.h.
			2/Lieut F. C. SMITH granted leave to U.K.	10.h.h.
			T/Lieut C. E. BARTER joined the Battalion.	10.h.h.
	22 Decr		Voluntary Church Services.	10.h.h.
			Battn Cross Country Run — winner Lt G.W. GIMBER.	10.h.h.
	23rd Decr		Salvage Operations continued.	10.h.h.
			Lieut Col A. CORRALL. M.O. (Comdg) returned from leave to U.K.	10.h.h.
			61 men proceeded to U.K. to be transferred to the Army Reserve Class (W).	10.h.h.

Army Form C. 2118.

WAR DIARY
or
INTELLIGENCE SUMMARY.
(Erase heading not required.)

6TH Sheet.

Place	Date	Hour	Summary of Events and Information	Remarks and references to Appendices
ST: HILAIRE	1918 23rd Dec		(Continued) and Smokers Concert between this Unit and "D" Batty 110th Brigade R.F.A. took place at 1730 hours.	
	24 Dec		No parade. The Battn commenced the Xmas Holidays. Lt GIMBER G.W. granted leave to U.K.	
	25 Dec		Voluntary Church Service. Men's dinner 12.30 hours. Menu Goose, Pork, Plum puddings, oranges and apples, beer. Concert 1730 hours Battn Concert 1930 hours. S.Q.Ts Mess dinner 1930 hours Officers Mess 2100 hours. A Battn dinner. Football match. Officers V Sgts. result Officers 4 Sergeants 2	
	26 Dec		No parade.	
	27 Dec		One company on Salvage operations to complete clearing the area of Salvage. Three Companies on ceremonial parade.	
	28 Dec		Battn Parade - Ceremonial drill.	

Army Form C. 2118.

WAR DIARY
or
INTELLIGENCE SUMMARY.

(Erase heading not required.)

4th Sheet.

Place	Date	Hour	Summary of Events and Information	Remarks and references to Appendices
	1918			
ST HILAIRE	29 Dec		2/Lt T.N.C. GOODWIN granted leave to U.K.	9/hr
			Lt E.C. CLEEVE granted leave to U.K.	9/hr
			The Battn cleaning up & fitting of equipment.	9/hr
LOUVIGNIES	30 Dec		The Battn moved from ST HILAIRE to LOUVIGNIES about	9/hr
9/00. VALENCIENNES			thirteen miles march.	
11/00.0.0.	31 Dec		Fitting up new billets.	9/hr

W.Caud
Lieut Colonel
Comdg. 11th Sherwood Foresters.

11 Stewart For
1st Sheet.
1st January 1919.

Army Form C. 2118.

WAR DIARY
or
INTELLIGENCE SUMMARY.
(Erase heading not required.)

Instructions regarding War Diaries and Intelligence Summaries are contained in F.S. Regs., Part II. and the Staff Manual respectively. Title pages will be prepared in manuscript.

Place	Date	Hour	Summary of Events and Information	Remarks and references to Appendices
	1919.			
LOUVIGNIES LES QUESNOY	1st Jany		Salvage operations commenced in new area	
VALENCIENNES (SHEET 1/100,000)			Despatches Extract from SIR DOUGLAS HAIG'S Despatch of Nov. 8th 1918, Submitting names deserving of special mention.	
			EAST KENT REGT. LT W.R. CORRALL. M.C. (T/MAJOR) att. 9th ROYAL SUSSEX REGT.	
	2nd Jan		Salvage operations continued	
	3rd Jan		Salvage operations continued	
	4th Jan		Salvage operations continued. 2nd Lieut R.J. CHESTER M.C. appointed to Battalion	
	5th Jan		Batts allotted to the Battn.	
	6th Jan		Batts allotted to the Battn. Ceremonial Drill	
			Extract from London Gazette of 30/12/18. NOTTS & DERBY REGT. 2nd LT F.C. SMITH (5th Battn.) T.F. to be Temp. Captain 6 Oct 29/18.	3 50
	7th Jan		Ceremonial Drill	
	8th Jan		Extract from M.S. List of appts. Commissions etc. No. 220:- NOTTS & DERBY REGT. 11th Battn. TEMPY LIEUT A.D. PARKIN, M.C. 16th Battn. to be Acting Captain whilst commanding a Coy. 7th Nov. 1918.	

WAR DIARY or INTELLIGENCE SUMMARY

Army Form C. 2118.
2nd Sheet.

Place	Date	Hour	Summary of Events and Information	Remarks and references to Appendices
	7th Jan		(Continued) Temp Lt (A/Capt) R W Black MC on ceasing to be acting Captain with effect 28th October 1918 relinquishes the pay & acting rank under the terms of G.R.O. 2678 dated 9th Oct 1917.	J.M.
	8th Jan		Ceremonial Drill. Lt SHORT W.E.R. joined the Batt'n	J.M.
	9th Jan		Ceremonial Drill.	J.M.
			Despatches. The f'ng have been mentioned in LORD CAVAN'S Despatch d/1st Jan 1919.	J.M.
			BIRD T/Capt B.W. M.C. 11th Batt'n	J.M.
			GIBSON T/Capt L.H. M.C. 11th Batt'n	J.M.
			HUDSON Capt (T/Lt Col) C.E. V.C. D.S.O. M.C. 1st Bn att 11th Bn	J.M.
			PEARSON T/Lt C.E. 11th Bn	J.M.
			SMITH 2/Lt F.C. att 11th Bn 5th Batt (T.F.)	J.M.
			WATTS T/Lt (acting Capt) H.A. 11th Bn.	J.M.
			BRANSTON 14586 Sgt (A/Bandmaster) J. 11th Bn	J.M.
			PINNIGER 18148 Sgt W.J. 11th Batt'n.	J.M.

Army Form C. 2118.

WAR DIARY
or
INTELLIGENCE SUMMARY.
(Erase heading not required.)

3RD SHEET

Instructions regarding War Diaries and Intelligence Summaries are contained in F. S. Regs., Part II. and the Staff Manual respectively. Title pages will be prepared in manuscript.

Place	Date	Hour	Summary of Events and Information	Remarks and references to Appendices
	10th Jan		Lecture by Mr R. TURNER. B.A Subject "Development & training of the BRITISH EMPIRE"	
	11th Jan		Ceremonial Drill	
			Ceremonial Drill	
			Salvage Operations	
	13th Jan		Ceremonial Drill	
	13th Jan		Ceremonial Drill	
			Salvage Operations	
	14th Jan		Ceremonial Drill	
	15th Jan		"Coronation" and "Trooping of the Colour"	
	16th Jan		Holiday	
	17th Jan		Salvage Operations	
	18th Jan		Salvage Operations 2nd Lt. C.G. TODD to U.K. as Conducting Officer	
	19th Jan		Church Parade	
	20th Jan		Salvage Operations	
	21st Jan		Salvage Operations	

WAR DIARY or INTELLIGENCE SUMMARY

Army Form C. 2118.

11th Cheshires

(Erase heading not required.)

Place	Date	Hour	Summary of Events and Information	Remarks and references to Appendices
Tournai	20th Jan		Lieut. Col. N.R. Corrall M.C. to U.K. for Course	
	21st		Capt. J.M. Marsh M.C. to U.K. relinquishing Officers	
			Capt. B.A. Whitacre C.F. taken on attached strength	
	22nd		Colony Operations and Parties	
	23rd		School Operations and Parties	
	24th		Salvage Operations and Parties	
	25th		Regimental Capt. Moore as "Demobilizing Recruiting"	
	26th		Church Parade	
	27th		Baths	
	28th		Baths	
	29th		Capt. I.G. Rivers M.C. Same, left Battalion	
			Capt. R.K. Menzor Rowe joined Battalion	
	29th Jan		Salvage Operations	
	30th Jan		2nd Battalion to hospital Railway work	
	31st Jan		Railway Operations	

J.C. Smith. Capt. r/Adjutant
for O.C. 11th Cheshire Fusiliers

11th Batt. SHERWOOD FORESTERS.
1st Sheet.

WAR DIARY
or
INTELLIGENCE SUMMARY.
(Erase heading not required.)

February 1919

Place	Date	Hour	Summary of Events and Information	Remarks and references to Appendices
LOUVIGNIES les QUESNOY	1919 Feb 1		Salvage. Concert by 25 Divisional Pierrots.	M.
VALENCIENNES	"2		Voluntary Church Parade. 2Lt H. Hemming to U.K. on leave.	M.
SHEET	"3		Batt's. Concert by Pierrots. Lt R. Murchie opened Br.	M.
	"4		Salvage and Bath.	M.
	"5		Voluntary Questions. 2Lt J.A. Austin rejoined from hospital.	M.
	"6		Salvage. Huntinno.	M.
	"7		Salvage. Questions.	M.
	"8		Salvage. Questions.	M.
	"9		Voluntary Church Parade. 2Lt A.E.L. Cornpton to U.K. on leave.	M.
	"10		Salvage. Questions. Capt. G.W. GIMBER & 2Lt P.S. Taylor rejoined Via U.K. for demobilization	M.
	"11		Salvage. Questions.	M.
	"12		Salvage. Questions. Lieut Col W.R. CORRALL M.C. (Course) and Capt. J.H. MARSH. M.C. rejoined Battalion from U.K.	M.
	"13		The Batt'n working on the fences of graves. Capt. F.C. SMITH proceeded to U.K. for demobilization	

WAR DIARY
INTELLIGENCE SUMMARY

Army Form C. 2118.

(Erase heading not required.)

Place	Date	Hour	Summary of Events and Information	Remarks and references to Appendices
HOUVIGNIES	13th		Extract from London Gazette dated February 10th 1919:—	
			Notts & Derbys Regt.	
			Temp: 2nd Lieut. to be Lieut. R.J. CHESTER M.C. previous next below	
			W. MEAKIN (Nov 20th 1915)	
			Temp: Major W.R. CORRALL M.C. (Temp Captain E. KENT Reg.)	
			E. KENT Regt. to command a Battalion and to be Temp. Lieut.	
			Colonel (Oct 29th 1918 with seniority April 11th 1918)	
	14th		2nd Lt S.P. HOWELL proceeded to UK for demobilisation	
			Salvage Operations	
	15th		Salvage Operations	
	16th		Church Parade. Lt. Col. W.R. CORRALL M.C. proceeded to UK & struck off strength	
	17th		The Battalion allotted huts at STEENWERCK. MAJOR R.M. GIBSON M.C. took over Command of the Battalion	
Sheet 71A	18th		The Battalion carried to HAUSSY	
	19th		The Battalion proceeded to IWUY	
	20th		Inspection Parade	
	21st		Inspection Parade	

WAR DIARY
INTELLIGENCE SUMMARY.
(Erase heading not required.)

Army Form C. 2118.

Place: **Sheet 3** H. Howard Vecco Cap

Place	Date	Hour	Summary of Events and Information	Remarks and references to Appendices
SHEET 51A	22nd Feb		Inspection Parades under Cos & Companies	
	23rd	"	Church Services. Inspection of billets by Commanding Officer.	
			The Corps Commander, under authority of His Majesty the King, awarded the Military Medal to the undermentioned N.C.Os. (Auth) DRO 4402 d/21/2/19.	
			10606 Sgt T. DALEY	
			36381 Cpl F. STAFFORD)	
	24th		Inspection Parades under Cos & Companies	
	25th		Salvage Operations.	
	26th		Salvage Operations.	
	27th		The Battn. allotted baths at IWUY	
	28th		Salvage Operations.	
			The Battn. received the Warning Order to move to CAMBRAI tomorrow 1st March 1919.	

COMMANDING 11th (S) BATTALION,
THE SHERWOOD FORESTERS.

www.ingramcontent.com/pod-product-compliance
Lightning Source LLC
Chambersburg PA
CBHW081240170426
43191CB00034B/1994